ABOUT

To mark a beginning is a great achievement however maintaining that is even a bigger one. So here we are with our limited resources negligible help and a humongous vision of putting ourselves out to the world. We at THE AUCTORES are endeavouring our best to provide arts and artists the exposure that is required. The plethora that has been missing. Is it hard? Yes. Will it take time? Yes. But be certain that it is possible in all its form and that exactly is the ideology behind THE AUCTORES. Let's join hands in our endeavour and bring to the world a distilled form of art that is, appreciated and recognized by all. I read somewhere that "art is the food to soul". And, I'm not certain what else will it take to make you ponder over the importance of arts in our day to day life. Enough about us, let's move on and to bring this magazine to spotlight, here's a brief on it. This is a collective work of many artists from rather different backgrounds. Yes, just like a pickle, a little bit of this and a tad bit of that. But however irregular it may sound in spite of the commonality it is the diversity that unites us. In this edition you will find variable sets of work and language which has been categorized as neatly as possible. In the first section you'll come across some mind blowing writings, an elegant mixture of some ecstatic poems and mind blowing essays. These're categorized firstly by language then by type. There are some true to art poems, emerging directly from the soul. We'd love to see you lose yourself in the symphony. We've also prepared some prompts via our social media and brings to you the best among scores of submissions. Post that you'll see perfection in the form of incredible fine arts, I really envy these artists. In the next section some photographers have displayed their talent in some amazing captures. And lastly, credit to our warriors of pen and brush. We sincerely hope this is going to be your best read of the month.

Write to us at support@theauctores.in
or visit : www.instagram.com/the_auctores/

EDITORIAL

In these times of global crisis, I wish you all a very healthy and hearty month. Hope you all are safe and sound. Days are tough and there's always a chance it might get tougher but as a unit we stand.

We do not go above, neither below, we go through. Because that is who we are and because that is what the moment demands. This world has shown an extreme level of tolerance, in these times of unbearable uncertainty and sky high intolerance. I bookmark these times as an example in prudence, awareness and helpfulness.

With a request to respect our public service staffs and officials, to support the efforts of our governments with maximum of your will and to save yourself from being a liability to your countries by staying in as much as possible, I'd like to continue.

I understand if you think the timing is inappropriate however my perception is, 'desperate times call for desperate measures'. With these words I bring food to your soul, something to take away your anxiety, something to dilute your dark thoughts and some to give wings to your imaginations. A remarkably good read for your current month.

I hereby present to you tenth edition of THE AUCTORES Monthly.
You can write to me at [divyamrakesh1@gmail.com]

JAI HIND
Regards
Divyam

ACKNOWLEDGEMENT

This E-book that you're about to read is similar to a handmade piece of clothing, in its essence. Weaved with care, line by line with the same commitment and enthusiasm. It is a collective work, so obviously it took efforts from many great souls and at many different fronts. I'd like to acknowledge the independent artists who were more than happy to share their work through our platform. They showed trust and faithfulness, and to my heart felt happiness it's poetic to announce that their trust has not been in vain. In this journey our mutual trust is a flag hoisting endlessly which shows us the basic values like humanity, warm heart, helpfulness, empathy and it most certainly is beautiful watching so many hues together.

Once again.

Thank you all!

CONTENTS

| THE AGONY OF THE NIGHT |

It's been night and silence was all over
My heart ached
as I felt something bad arriving
I jumped in my bed to sleep,
But the voices started raising
N I knew it was just the beginning.
Within seconds the voices
turned into yells and screams
Yes! They were fighting again.
A shiver ran down my body
As I curled up myself blocking my ears with my hands
But it didn't help much
As the voices echoed
in every corner of the room
Before I could realise anything
tears slipped down my eyes
I was silently gulping down my sobs
So that no one could hear me cry
My heartbeat was increasing with every yell and scream I heard
All I could do was pray
that it passes away soon.
Finally, Silence took over again
I could hear the clock ticking and
my heart still thumping.
I knew the storm outside had calmed down but
the storm inside me had just began
I tried to sleep
but sleep was far away from me
I just stared at the sky,
as tears made their way down
A river of thoughts flooded in my mind
making me cry even more
I was tired and exhausted and finally sleep took over me
and I closed my eyes
letting the last drop of tear
slip down in sigh.

– Amisha Colaco

01

| THE WOODS OF PLEASURE |

In the deep woods
There lays the mind
For the city lights that keep getting me blind
My eyes are deep and dark
It's been years since I have smiled with an arc .

Those deep shades of the oak
The high-pitched quawks of the toad .
The profound air of the woods that nourishes
And prevents the ache of happiness , the citylights garnishes .

The melodies of the cuckoo
That makes my anxiety bid adieu
The mesmerizing smell of the cedar
I wonder if there's a better healer !

It's the friendly nature's room
That makes each of my nerves bloom
The crazy cricket's melancholy
I wonder it's the reason , for the nature's so holy .

The blues of the sky that hail
The miracles of the nature that prevail
The greys of the clouds
That praise the blessings of the nature aloud .

The gentle morning dew that tickles
Each of my veins and tenderly trickles .
The glorious soars of the eagle
It's all a blessing for a man so feeble .

The lone woods that happily enwraps
As I find peace in it's lap .
And besides the inner pleasure
There remained utter sadness , for thy the helpless nature .

– Vardaan Vikram Singh

02

| RUINED EULOGIES |

Vibrations of frosted
memories
of a midsummer night
are showing
their significance
while I am swallowing pills of reality.
It's like somewhere in between
monochromes and rainbows
where the vibrant colours
of summers are buried deep within somewhere unknown.
The huntress in me who once chased the dreams
is now being blindfolded and
slashed by the
sullen thunders on the horizon,
solitude engulfs her as she dared to dream .
When sunlight bathes these palms
It seems like
my hands are covered with yellow paints and mouth sewed
with ruined eulogies,
these stitches
behind the dark shadows of
my sun dappled palms,
screams but in silence
like the abraded and broken bricks of an abandoned
place,
once called home,
and their hireath for the glorious days!
I, the defeated huntress
let the glaciers of those frosted memories, run
down and down from my eyes,
in soulful symphonies-
as an ode to a place,
once called our peace haven,
and now an empty mausouleum.

– Poulomi Sarkar

MODERN DAY INVASION

AN ARTICLE BY <u>NISHA ANKUSH</u> & <u>DIVYAM RAKESH</u>

Source - Al-Arabiya news house

Thousands of faces, all hopeless. Kids crying their hearts out and so does the adults. Screaming to save them from the impending doom. Approaching every foreign face in a hope of getting asylum, in a failed attempt to dodge the said doom. Chaos all around, parents trying to ensure a safe passage for their young ones at the least, if not for them. Such was the scene outside Afghan Int. Airport, these past few weeks.

How did the country find itself on a brink of a civil war, overnight ?

I'm sorry, it wasn't overnight, US took 4 presidents, thousands of lives, trillion of dollars and 20 years to replace Taliban, with Taliban. Let me start by breaking down the timeline for you, so let us start from the beginning.

> "US took 4 presidents, thousands of lives, trillion of dollars and 20 years to replace Taliban, with Taliban."

Taliban is a Pashto word meaning students or seekers. Taliban is another name foe 'Wahabism' & 'Mujahideen'. 'Wahhabism' refers to the followers of Mohammad Ibn Abd al-Wahab who started reform movement in (1703-1792) Najd in central Arabia, advocating a purging of widespread practice such as veneration od saints and pilgrimages to their tombs and shrines. This is the strictest form of Sunni- Islam which adheres to the Athari theology. In essence, in the orthodox movement of the religion, the texts of the Quran and Hadith is accepted without asking "how".

'Jihad' is another term for struggle on behalf of Islam/Allah or Islamic community, Arabic term for the ones who wage jihad is 'Mujahideen'. In 18th century few modernists' thinkers such as Shah Wali Allah considered Muslim rule important for the revival of Islamic society. Thus, Muslims who refrained the expansion of the Marathas, Jatts and Sikh armies into Muslim areas were considered 'Mujahideen'. Later in 19th century, movement of Sayyid Ahmed Baralawi fought both Sikh expansion and British paramountcy in India.

In 20th century, in Iran the 'Mujahideen-e-Khalq', a group of Islamic and Marxist ideologies, engaged in a long-term guerrilla war against the leadership of Islamic republic.

In Afghanistan a guerrilla group, that opposed the invading soviet forces and eventually toppled the AF communist government during Afghan war (1978-'92), is termed as Mujahideen.

Source – Google/media houses on the web.

Post 9/11 the US decided to deploy NATO troops in AF as their counter terrorism plan objectives were to, Get Bin Laden, Defeat Taliban, reconstruction and support to create a well established Afghan army. That was the start of 20 years long struggle in the country. Bin Laden was killed in an Op (Neptune spear by US navy Seals in Abbottabad) in Pakistan. Post that troops remained intact to support counter-terrorism efforts by Afghan army, government and training the elite AA to fight terrorism.

Forwarding ahead a decade in 2021, Joe Biden governed US decided to withdraw US & NATO troops. No more on ground support. Owing to the decision Taliban, which was never extinct but somehow managed to remain below the government's radar, rose with a substantial force. Probably with a foreign influence, started targeting and capturing cities one by one until the day even the capital city, Kabul, fell. However, the AF Int. airport remained out of their control, as US troops were using it for evacuation and withdrawal.

Now, coming to the question, why this withdrawal resulted in such an elaborated chaos? – to keep it short and precise,

Source – Google/media houses on the web.

1) Fear of transition of power once the chain of command broke. It should have been a gradual and stepwise action. Sudden withdrawal of troops caused a power vacuum and Taliban rushed in, to fill the void.

2) Local government was only based on urban areas/population, couldn't gather the confidence of the hearts and minds of afghanis, while Taliban grew itself in the rural areas of the country to remain off the radar and made itself stronger over the years.

Their propaganda was mainly based on killing of the innocent in air strikes and others in local clashes with NATO or US troops.

3) Corruption to grass root level. Not only this US supported government couldn't gather the confidence, but it was also corrupt to their bones. In a report by there are many schools in afghanistan which exists but merely on paper. Students, on paper; teachers, on paper, however there is no actual existence of these outside the pieces of paper which is used to cover up scores worth billions of dollars received in donation from International agencies and thus was used the concept of ghost schools. Same went for the local armed forces, The Afghan national army

or ghost soldiers. The ones that exist only in records and theories but they are no more than merely a theory. And hence Afghan Army, a formidable force on papers with world class armaments and equipment and world class training never stood a chance against Taliban.

In a recent press conference Taliban brought themselves to show a new face of the said militants however this remains merely propaganda as on ground the

Source - Google/media houses on the web.

2021 Taliban seem no different than 1996 Taliban in action. Sharia was still there; women are barred from a lot of day-to-day activities and such. Governments from all around the globe are discussing if they're to give recognition to this government or not. In my honest opinion a government formed on gunpoint is no different than a dictatorship and therefore shouldn't be considered a viable form of government. But keeping in mind the government established by the US was no more than a puppet and was put there for the sole purpose of satisfying their trade needs and extract profit out of the given demography serves the same purpose but under a disguise.

Now what is most important is that the people should have a say in it above all.

Source - Google/media houses on the web.

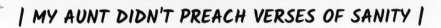

| MY AUNT DIDN'T PREACH VERSES OF SANITY |

They say, she used to write
poems to her beloved,
and rants to her
long lost lover.
she sent those to him
every day, every night,
seeking betrayal wrapped
in envelopes of disbelief
instead the khaki-adorned man
left postcards of intimacy.

she carried grasslands
within and swept away
twigs which carved
imprints like walls of monastery,
trembling over the stack of hay,
my aunt never apologised for mischiefs
her ghosts perpetrated.

now her poems are
treasured in museums
of middle-east
embracing the walls which transcribe her thesis of long living in arabic dialect.

they whispered to me,
your aunt's body is
as pious as Ganges,
though
her ashes were dipped
in melancholy,
skin burnt to the
fumes of misery
as her soul ached while
leaving the territory.

– Chehak Mehra

| THINGS WENT PEAR-SHAPED |

So the British saying goes—
meaning, I guess, they bottomed
out. Of pears, though, such sweetness
comes. Money's, Van Gogh's, Cezanne's
hold the sun in all its shifting shades.

We had a line pear tree in the backyard
of our first house in Roosevelt, Long Is.
I remember staring up at its spindly spokes
when I was almost drowning at the bottom
of our kiddie pool. I felt free, for the strain
of seconds that span a lifetime, before being
plucked to breath. I was pear-shaped, until
the mangoes grew & my hour-glass profile in-
stilled life made me dangerous, too tasty,
too good & evil for the addiction prone.

Maybe it was a pear, in the Garden, that bent her?
Dew drop, from the fruit, fell on the forked tongue
of the spitting basilisk; becoming an amuse-bouche
before that first, fateful bite. We always see hope,
in that particular tint of yellow, or genius or insanity.
When most ripe, we coast teeth into flesh, like a spoon
over sherbet curls ice. It melts down the gullet, unaware
of the acidic breakdown at hand. This metaphor, too,
may break.

The other day, at the fridge, I felt a familiar pear-
shaped presence, a kind sent to follow the trauma
damned, pursing to hiss me toward stilling my life.
I sang, instead, in a language unlearned—ancient
& angelic—brushing past it with a wonder, working
power of song & dance & light—that certain slant of light.

– Kristy "Kiki" Johnson

08

| A SONNET TO THE TRUTHFUL HEART |

I have a heart with the power
Of truth inside its every chamber;
Thou art falsehood that is lower
To anything even to dying timber;
My mouth cannot utter a word
Amidst the cruel sinners of earth;
The tongue of me maketh a sword
Which doth cure the global wrath.
Shall I need to curse my kind heart?
I will not do it for anything, at last;
The truth hath gift'd an elegant art
That look'd young and act'd fast.
I never forgive thee for my tragic fall,
The truthful heart, thou art always tall.

-Mr.V.Heymonth Kumar

| IMPORTANCE |

I am not here to see my worth through someone else's eyes,
even though it took me years of frazzled sorting,
for me to finally realize...
Those that gauge their importance on another person's opinion,
will never find pure peace inside and will always feel a smaller size...
Where our problems overflow and rise,
is when we aren't able to recognize
the patterns that we repeat, in disguise, for our own demise!
The best that can happen to a tattered soul,
is to be pushed SO HARD, you stand up and say "Hell NO"
and watch "People Pleasing" minimize!
We can take back our integrity from the
suppression of any demented way of life,
self created or led into, but no longer consider to be wise...

- Tracey Ross

MONOTONES

Sudiksha Ghosh

THE POSITIVE OMEN

This artwork of mine shows an old woman wearing a kashmiri shawl intricately embroidered. She is as positive as the embroidery of her shawl and as bold as her eyes. No matter how old she is, from within, she's as pure as the moon.

Anastasia Smith

ANGEL OF DUALITY

This is a monochromatic graphite and pen drawing of a female angel with one white wing and the other a black wing, showing from her bare back . She is walking up the remains of stairs which is gradually crumbling into ruins and ash , while staring out into the smoky neverwhere.

Sudiksha Ghosh

This artwork of mine shows the majestic view of the Varanasi Ghar in the dawn. Its a mixed media artwork, using pens and colours. I've used to colour orange-red for the flags as it is the holy colour of Hindus mainly and is seen a lot in such Ghats in India.

| UNSOLICITED DEEAMS |

I would sit on the terrace and watch the stars
No one to disturb but the moon
The glittering tin roofs in the dark would pinch
My eyes like the bright light in the sunny noon

I would shuffle myself to parry it off
Push my back to the edge to keep it away
But thin moon light crept from the corners
Unwillingly in the charm of its magic, I would sway

In the dreams influenced by this enchanting spell
Stars would run, dance and joyfully scream
Charmed me without the flick of moon
Alas, it was nothing but a beautiful dream

Who woke me up!
Was it the drop of dew on my face
Or the drizzle that the breeze drew along
My eyes opened only to find the clouds that
Eclipsed the moon, my stars and my song...

– Syed Sajjad Qadri

| SULK |

my palate was sour,
I didn't prefer to utter a bit of air
because it was throttled by the vicious time
thus my frivolous sense was on the stride
to brimmed the vacant panes
with the sulking odor of per perplexing phrases
in the fiction, although it was no match
to those who were chaperoned
by the phenomenal meticulous souls,
nevertheless, it comforted my fouls.

– Aditi kumari

| TELL ME YOUR STORY |

Tell me your story.
No, not what is your job or your hobbies.
Tell me what scares you,
tell me about your pain,
tell me when did your heart
last feel light.
Tell me your deepest desires,
your hopes and dreams.
Tell me about the shadows
and what does your soul crave,
tell me how to love you.
Sit with me,
tell me your story.

- Barbara Gianguitto

| DELUSION UNDERNEATH |

Once, the king of ocean - killer whale;
Mailed me to make match in real,
Salmon's shock for changes in him,
Dreadly distressed as to pair with whim;
I not uttered a word, instead headed
With stiffened back with least hope lead;
Heads straight, hands wrapped in sour
Pricked about the future bearing a heavy sore.

Addressed me, "my dear beauty blush"---
I am not intent to take away your flesh.
He pleaded to pleasant his obnoxious life;
I gently replied, "I'll stay with thine as wife",
Though I can see the world by climbing peaks,
But thy heart is the world of mine that lasts.
I sprouted up with sigh out, beads of sweat!
That hawled me as delusion drowned in threat.

- Sneha Kannusamy.

13

| TWIST |

Everywhere is full of big essences
Crafted in the unbendable system
A nowhere quenching and burning ecstasies
Fast crackerjacks manufacture ways out
Testing the hypothesis of history
Making fragile the path of liberation
People wonder fearing the turn
Though they are close to getting it
Yet they are scared
This might just be another animal-farm
They wrap their lives around
As they doubt they have got it.

Liberation calls "come here darlings"
The sweetness of the Universe
Come have tasty portions of the Universe's love
In abundance
Waste no time as Time may close the gate of chance
Sages think they know everything
This program you escape from
This newness you head on to, if you do
I assure you they do not exist in understanding of it
Do not last one day in this horror blooming
Accept the plea of destiny, enjoy purpose
The Universe invites you to merry.

– Makinde Kehinde Margret

14

| HOPE |

Hope is
The translucent angel
The stowaway in the baggage of the lonely
Silently waiting to open her wings
While she waits to be summoned
By the dreamweaver

– Debie

THE HENNA ARTIST

A BOOK REVIEW BY <u>SEJUTI MAJUMDAR</u>

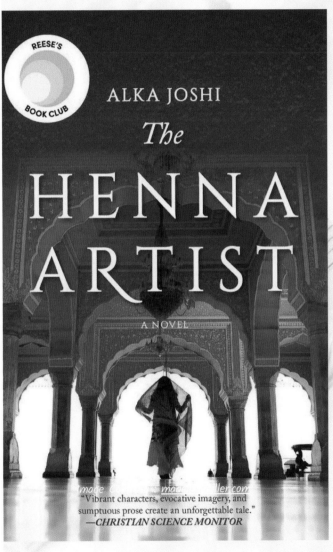

> "Vibrant characters, evocative imagery, and
> sumptuous prose create an unforgettable tale."
> —*CHRISTIAN SCIENCE MONITOR*

Her world takes a hit and everything she built starts to fall apart when her 13 year old sister Radha shows up about whose existence Laxmi wasn't aware.

I loved the storyline and the writing style was excellent. Throughout the book kept me hooked. The character portrayal was good though I have some doubts about Radha. The clever ways through which Laxmi handled her life and the way she had to struggle in between everything that was thrown at her was a really emotional journey to read.

Overall reading this book has been a pleasant experience for me. I am excited to read the next part and also the show that is coming adapted from the book.

If you are planning to read this book don't delay.

Book Name : The Henna Artist
Author : Alka Joshi
Publisher : HarperCollins

| SOUL CONNECTION |

Wondering what
brings me here
It's the connection
between you and me
I'm holding even now
It may connect
or reject a few
But my love will
remain to the core
I didn't force
anything between us
Everything happened
on it's own
We met through
natural vibrations
Now, I celebrate it
as a happy occasion!

– Shweta Mahani

| GERI DÖNÜŞ OLSA |

I seek refugee in your eyes Of melancholy.
When we danced rays of sunlight lit our dark rooms,
I wore nothing but liberation.
I became the woman
I always dreamed of being in the garden of Eden.
And now you ask me to maybe turn back.

what a glorious love story
I belong to the land of the deserts
but how would you know the sandstorms
I carry in my heart
so I turn back.

he told me to maybe turn back.

– Hayatt Askim

| OF SMILES AND SUFFERINGS |

I run my dried fingers on top of the most fresh wound, out of the sea of cuts on my left hand. it still has blood, dried yet red. blood. i smell it. i decide not to like it. i laugh at my own misery. i used to fear blood so much just one year back and now i dance in the pool of redness, without much thinking. i still don't like the smell though. never did.

oh! i remember i have to take my medicine. the anti depressant. i pretend to forget about it again. anyway, they are not helping either. if anything, i am deterioting, heading towards a deep dark dead end without any hope of light. a dead end which will swallow me up within a few days. or maybe few hours? who knows? i laugh again. this time on my confusions, which are eating up my last bit. the tiny pieces, the darkness left behind.

I look at the wall of my dark room. a smiling picture greets me from a distance. ma, papa and me. small, happy us. just last year. where did that smile disappear? i flinch at my own question. i remember how happy i was on that day. my 25th birthday. that long drive, the flickering street light, the soft music, the laughter. and boom! everything finished in one go. my whole world crumbled leaving me with the only ability to breath. ma and papa did not come back after that. neither did my smile. nor my happiness. my world stopped from that day onwards. that was the day i took the first step towards this maze, hurting myself with a small blade. the person who cried even when a small pin went into her skin, now danced with cuts and scars all over. but what do i do? i try to stop myself. or maybe i don't. i like to believe i do. i do try. but the darkness, the loneliness is powerful than my already shaken will. i fear my own self now, my dull soul, my beating heart. and. and my life. and my unloved, lonely, colourless life.

- Aditi Archita Khataniar

17

INTRICATE ARTWORKS

Surekha Biswas

If I sleep at night, when will I watch the moon?

Vanshika Chopra

OOPSIE DAISY

| WHERE I REMAIN |

Skies of ruby and orange zest
As the sun tucks itself beneath the cityscape.
Shadows crawl upon cement lands,
Streaking darkness before night.
Buzzing arises from towering steel lamps.
And when their light pierces the dense grunge,
They find me there—
I am bundled within my coat, perceiving myself
As rubbish abandoned upon the streets.
I hunker between the shade and light,
Venturing onward into the enigma.
The coldness of darkness swaddles me
Blood has foregone nourishing my limbs,
Retreating into my throbbing heart.
Absent wishes contribute to my dismay
As I remain wondering the grim streets
Under the polluted evening skies and rust-colored illumination.

- S.C. Patterson

| OCEANS OF TIME |

Life ebbs and flows with the oceans of time
Sweeping you off your feet towards the deadening undercurrent below
As the Wheels of Fate slowly take away your prime
Deeper into the murky waters we disappear under that cruel tow
Losing more of who we are each day that clock ticks
Crimson starting to flow around us as the jagged rocks nick
The vulnerable flesh that contains our essence, our dying soul
Spiraling further into that neverending black hole
From birth to death the cycle never ends
And this existence is just on loan, until the afterlife we ascend
The conscious mixing with the unconscious creating pings of doubt
Of what is real and what is just an illusion
As our sanity begins to black out
Giving into the shadows of delusion
Until the last of our electrical impulses flatline
Because we finally ran out of the concept of time.

- Sara Brunner

19

THE BELL JAR

A BOOK REVIEW BY <u>SWATI MISHRA</u>

Book: The Bell Jar
Author: Sylvia Plath
Review: Swati Mishra

One of the most comforting feelings is to find people like us who too have gazillion of 'eccentric' thoughts popping in their mind at irregular intervals. But if you find the world too uptight to own that the bell jar stifles them at times too, turn to this book, the protagonist-Esther Greenwood is the literary manifestation of the quirkiness that exists in all of us. She wants to live in the countryside as well as city, at times she feels that life in Europe and tryst with lovers can provide her enough content for writing a novel and at times she wants to settle in Chicago with a brand new identity and have lots of children. She makes plans after plans like 'scatty rabbits' and she feels inadequate among the accomplished. She is a lot like us and we are a lot like her.

Mental agony is not apparent and hence maybe snubbed by many but the journey of Esther delineates the desperate need of the sufferers, why they will do anything to exchange it with any form of physical pain rather than living with the fact that something was wrong with their head. After Esther's stay in asylum, her mom terms the whole thing as 'a bad dream' but Esther knew that forgetfulness might numb the experience in the way snow covers a landscape but the landscape is still very much there, very much like the experiences we go through, they become a part of us, we cannot escape from our own self.

And of course there are people like Buddy Williard (ex-lover) in the world, whose biggest concern was whom Esther will marry after she had been in a mental health institution. The hypocrite world and its rules that drives us insane also demands Certificate of Sanity to be included has been depicted poignantly by the author.

Well I must say, it might be a difficult read for some group of readers as books with non-linear plots comparatively are and that too when at points caviar, place-card or bathroom tubs have found elaborate description. Almost every chapter begins with somewhere in the middle of something and then traced to the origin of the incident and the end is neither happy nor sad (except the suicide of Joan), much like life itself, that goes on till the time you find yourself saying the words -" I took a deep breath and listened to the old brag of my heart. I am, I am, I am."

| ODE TO THE CITIES |

New times
New rhymes
Urban glamgirls
Start new tribes
Paris London Rome Dubai
Forming new hashtag allies.

Where're you from?
I am from Berlin,
I spend my days discovering new art
with a coffee mug
In my hand
and AirPods
in my ears.
I don't drink liters of beer
No more German potato salad for lunch
I prefer avo on toast
And eggs benedict for my Sunday brunch.
Just like my friend from New York.
I am not different from her.

Cities created a new caste
We love our polluted air and waking up around noon.
We are not German British American Spanish Russian
Anymore.
We are URBAN(e).

– Inna Rothmann

21

| SILENCE |

A silence between us
Spoke a million words
That we both loved each other
but could not face the world
So it had to end.

– Shuchi Batra

| BEING THERE FOR YOU |

Be the guiding light.
There will be a time in life when everything seems blurry and dark. It could be the end of cycles and the moment for a new beginning to embark. Losing homes, losing loved ones, and things that mattered once. Soon needs to rebuild the city with great power, potential, and eloquence. Their faith will get shattered repetitively but tell them we shall not leave the fight. If the warmth is missing, provide them with hope, strength, and a hug so tight.

Be the inspirational rain.
Season after season, the plants stopped growing without the shower from the sky, the land became wild and barren. The wanderers of the oceans and the seas lost their way listening to the loud wailing sound of a Siren. The bare necessities need to be feed, not only for the state of survival but to progress and compete. Let them know, there exists a world beyond human needs where they have to work creatively hard and repeat. Henceforth, the start of a new era, an era of growth and prosperity. A place of the time where the herd of humans could come together and magnify their divinity.

Be the hope for a brighter future.
Educate their children to understand the mysteries of the world and how it works. With mannerism and morality, teach them to be bold and courageous to discover life's wonders and perks. Provide them a secure environment where they could flourish and get inspired every day. No matter what the journey of living would hold for them, nothing could ever get in the middle of their play. Skilled parenting and effortless loving will always be there to endure. The ease at connecting and expressing every mindset shall become a part of the cure.

- Bhagyashree Besra

22

MADHUBANI & MANDALA WORKS

LORD HANUMAN

CATCHING THE SUN

According to Valmiki's Ramayana, an ancient Hindu epic, Lord hanuman in his childhood was hungry and saw the rising red colored sun. Mistaking it for a ripe fruit, he leapt up to eat it. Tried to show this part of the legend through this Dot Mandala painting on canvas.

Parul Mangal

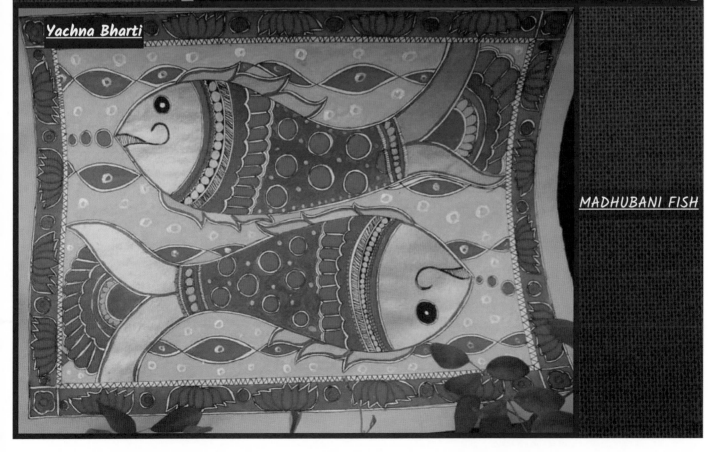

Yachna Bharti

MADHUBANI FISH

| PERFECT |

My window shews the travelling clouds,
Leaves spent, new seasons, alter'd sky,
The making and the melting crowds:
The whole world passes; I stand by.

They do not waste their meted hours,
But men and masters plan and build:
I see the crowning of their towers,
And happy promises fulfill'd.

And I - perhaps if my intent
Could count on prediluvian age,
The labours I should then have spent
Might so attain their heritage,

But now before the pot can glow
With not to be discover'd gold,
At length the bellows shall not blow,
The furnace shall at last be cold.

Yet it is now too late to heal
The incapable and cumbrous shame
Which makes me when with men I deal
More powerless than the blind or lame.

No, I should love the city less
Even than this my thankless lore;
But I desire the wilderness
Or weeded landslips of the shore.

I walk my breezy belvedere
To watch the low or levant sun,
I see the city pigeons veer,
I mark the tower swallows run

Between the tower-top and the ground
Below me in the bearing air;

– Pakhi

24

Then find in the horizon-round
One spot and hunger to be there.

And then I hate the most that lore
That holds no promise of success;
Then sweetest seems the houseless shore,
Then free and kind the wilderness,

Or ancient mounds that cover bones,
Or rocks where rockdoves do repair
And trees of terebinth and stones
And silence and a gulf of air.

There on a long and squared height
After the sunset I would lie,
And pierce the yellow waxen light
With free long looking, ere I die.

| UNSAVED |

I raised the alarm
But no one responded
I raised the alarm
Still no one came
I raised the alarm
My screams were silenced
I raised the alarm
As I lay in your shame
I raised the alarm
Maybe violence is deafening?
I raised the alarm
Just got more of the same
I raised the alarm
I waited and waited
I raised the alarm
Tucked away the stains
I raised the alarm
I raised..., I raised...
I... Walked away
And never raised it again

– Renaria B.

| PERSEVERANCE |

Inspired by a vision a soul sees every morning when it wakes up to see another day , in the time and dimension of this galaxy , it wonders if it would be able to make it to the old days , because it heard it's grandparents talk that" No wonder life is hard and with misery , every person should find small snippets because in those wrinkly skin and grey hair , there would be experiences worth seeing and living.

Back again
Not caring
to wonder
the jubilant
Strokes of shades
those colours bring
to the heart
that chose to be
Dull and grey,
with timely
knocks of hypocrisy
on the door
of solitude
which has rusted now
but not yet
attacked by termites
it has not fallen yet
but shaken,
and timid
to the force of the
Wind,
that comes around
to break it,
into pieces
That wouldn't
be found
No where, if lost,
no matter how many attempts
the other hand takes
but repairing is beyond

\- Aastha Sharma

26

the leap of intentions
and such hearts and
are buried in a
Coffin of denial
With no keys
to confessions
would you piece me back
with the same
love and affection ?
just stay near the door,
I won't fall,
it's a game of survival,
I might not have the key
but I know it All.

| UNPLANNED |

Mother flung the word unplanned
at me like a frisbee, expecting
me to catch it in my mouth
and join in with her game.

Contraception had failed
and I was the result
of this ugly equation. Ugly
as leftover snow mixed with mud,

ugly as the scalloped sole
of a shoreline at low tide.
Ugly as the naked mole rat,
the blobfish, giant salamander.

Every puddle is a broken mirror,
every reflection an uncomfortable
realisation. I'm a jigsaw waiting
for the box to scoop me up
while the telephone growls
like a protective wolf.

- Christian Ward

27

SAVE FARMERS SAVE DEMOCRACY

AN ARTICLE BY NISHA ANKUSH

Source - Google/media houses on the web.

Globally known Farmers' agitation against three acts passed by the government of India has taken next level form. June 26 is observed as " save farmers save democracy" by Farmers' union. Farmers' protest and their adamant decision signify their right to live and work freely in democratic nation. However, government takes this as anti-nation activity. Many have given this agitation name of Khalistani and terrorists. Is it all true? The Head of the family makes rule and regulations to benefit all members of the house. What if few members have their own mindset and are adamant to not accept changes? It is no wrong to speak your mind and object against you don't

want to follow. Though, we must not be violent in our deeds. Such is the inner dilemma of today's youth towards this ongoing protest of farmers against government's three laws.

The laws are: The Farmers' Produce Trade and Commerce (Promotion and Facilitation) Act, The Essential Commodities (Amendment) Act and The

> "Don't let your bread come under control of these big corporations. They make you purchase "free" water for INR 20. Imagine what will be the cost of wheat and pulses which is seasoned with our hard work?"

Farmers (Empowerment and Protection) Agreement on Price Assurance and Farm Services Act. (According to an article published in Times of India on December 15, 2020)

The three laws had first come in the month of June as the three Ordinances before being approved by Parliament during the Monsoon Session by a voice vote. The Farmers' Produce Trade and Commerce (Promotion and Facilitation) Act provides for setting up a mechanism allowing the farmers to sell their farm produces outside the

Agriculture Produce Market Committees (APMCs). Any license-holder trader can buy the produce from the farmers at mutually agreed prices. This trade of farm produces will be free of mandi tax imposed by the state governments. The Farmers (Empowerment and Protection) Agreement of Price Assurance and Farm Services Act allows farmers to do contract farming and market their produces freely.

The Essential Commodities (Amendment) Act is an amendment to the existing Essential Commodities Act. This law now frees items such as food grains, pulses, edible oils and onion for trade except in extraordinary (read crisis) situations.

As per information published in Financial Express, The Minimum Support Price or the MSP is commonly known as the way of protecting the farmers in India from the uncertainties of the markets as well as those of the natural kind. A 'safety net' for the farmers, the MSP is the core of the agricultural revolution that saw India transforming from a food-deficient to a food-surplus nation. Over the years, the MSP has helped the farmers in India to stave off the effects of financial fluctuations. At present, the Centre provides the MSP for 23 crops. These include cereals such as bajra, wheat, maize, paddy barley, ragi and jowar; pulses like tur, chana, masur, urad and moong; oilseeds such as safflower, mustard, niger seed, soyabean, groundnut, sesame and sunflower. The MSP also covers commercial crops of raw jute, cotton, copra and sugarcane.

Is MSP legal? Short answer – No. While Centre has been providing the MSP to the wheat and paddy farmers since mid-60s to tide over the food crisis, the fact remains that the MSP doesn't have any legal stature. The working of the MSP system has been such over the years that it benefits only a handful of farmers at all-India level. The Shanta Kumar committee set up by the Narendra Modi government in 2015 said only six per cent farmers benefit from the MSP regime.

Some economists have called the MSP system of India one of the costliest government food procurement programmes in the world.

The rising food bill under the existing MSP system of the government translates into pressure on the fiscal deficit in the annual budget. This is the reason why every government in the past several years has tried to find a way out.

Second issue of Farmers' protest is the amendment of the Agricultural Produce Marketing Committee (APMC) Act. According to Krishi Jagran, Agricultural Produce Market Committees (APMC) is the marketing boards established by the state governments in order to eliminate the exploitation incidences of the farmers by the intermediaries, where they are forced to sell their produce at extremely low prices.

All the food produce must be brought to the market and sales are made through auction. The marketplace i.e., Mandi is set up in various places within the states. These markets geographically divide the state. Licenses are issued to the traders to operate within a market. The mall owners, wholesale traders, retail traders are not given permission to purchase the produce from the farmers directly. There are around 7,000 APMC mandis across the country from where the government agencies including the Food Corporation of India (FCI) purchase farm produces. However, in a practical sense, only the paddy and wheat are procured by the FCI and other agencies for the want of fund. The FCI sells these food grains to the Below Poverty Line (BPL) families through the Public Distribution System (PDS) at a concessionary rate. This is loss-making or welfare-oriented practice. Rising procurement by means the FCI warehouses are overflowing, and rising

MSP means that the FCI cannot sell its stocks in the international market at a profit. The government compensates the FCI for its losses, and at times sells food grains to some countries under an agreement.

Government has proposed written assurance of MSP to the farmers, yet they are not ready to accept any amendments in the acts. Moreover, the Centre is likely to send a new proposal over Agricultural Produce Market Committees (APMCs) to protesting farmers after farmer's rejected government's proposal on MSP and stayed firm on scrapping farm laws. This is the scenario of great protest going on in the great democratic nation, India. Middle class society of the country is affected the most by any decision

Source - Google/media houses on the web.

taken by the government. A family with an average monthly income can be aware of the news and other things going around. Albeit, they don't have time to favour who they want to. Or, we should say, they are struggling everyday meeting daily expenses with limited resources. Are these people for whom our dear farmers are protesting? One in the crowd said to a news reporter, "Don't let your bread come under control these big corporations. They make you purchase "free"

water for INR 20. Imagine what will be the cost of wheat and pulses which is seasoned with our hard work?" Average person is thinking and waiting for the fate's command.

MSP means that the FCI cannot sell its stocks in the international market at a profit. The government compensates the FCI for its losses, and at times sells food grains to some countries under an agreement.

Government has proposed written assurance of MSP to the farmers, yet they are not ready to accept any amendments in the acts. Moreover, the Centre is likely to send a new proposal over Agricultural Produce Market Committees (APMCs) to protesting farmers after farmer's rejected government's proposal on MSP and stayed firm on scrapping farm laws. This is the scenario of great protest going on in the great democratic nation, India. Middle class society of the country is affected the most by any decision

Source - Google/media houses on the web.

Until latest news :

- Around 300 protestants were briefly detained in Gautam Buddha Nagar district near Noida authority office on 1st of this month.
- There has been a lathi charge on the protesting farmers in Moga, Punjab, in which many farmers have been injured. After the lathi charge, angry farmers also pelted stones at the police, in which many policemen were injured.

ROOM FOR PHOTOGRAPHS

A MOTHER OWNS TWO HEARTS ❤

Souhardya Dutta

Kay.

WINTER MORNING IN BEAUTIFUL AUSTRALIA

Greetje Siekmans

NIGHTFALL ON THE CANAL

LIKE A PALE VIOLET TONED LILAC SHE IS

Omair

CHAPTER-3

The whole day Smrithi can't stop thinking about the incident. She will not be active in anything whatever she is doing. Siya will be observing her and she will think to speak to Smrithi in person so after lunch she will go to her.

Smrithi will be arranging her room and suddenly when she turns back, she will see Siya.

Smrithi: Oh, it's you I got scared can't you just knock the door before you come in?

Siya: will sit on her bed and will have a weird scary smile.

Smrithi: why are you smiling like that?

Siya: keeps smiling.

Then someone will knock the door. Smriti ignores her and goes and opens the door it will be Siya.

Siya: hey, can we talk for some time?

Smrithi turns and sees for Siya in her room but she will not find her.

Siya: hey smriti

Smrithi: No no, I don't want to talk to anyone please leave me (and starts crying).

Then Siya walks in and holds Smrithi's hands and hug her and console her

Siya: why are you crying? please don't cry, I'm there for you.

Smrithi: I want to go back home I'm scared; I'm scared to be here.

Siya: Can you tell me what's happening with you. We will try to solve it. How can we leave our dreams because we are scared? (Siya will look in to Smrithi's eyes and tell her all these words). Then Smrithi

starts telling to her whatever happened and till now.

Smrithi: Can you believe whatever is happening to me is real?

Siya: Of course, I believe in you. I'll think of something and we will solve this. Give sometime I'll try to make things alright if it's not working, we will leave okay.

Smrithi: Okay.

Siya: now you stop crying and come we will just go for a walk.

Smrithi: okay.

Siya will ask Nayana and Riya also to join for the walk. So, everyone will be walking around the streets. While coming back to house opposite their house there will be another home but no one stays there while passing by that home Siya will hear a voice calling her name in a scary tone.

Siya turn towards that home and stops there for a second other girls will continue walking towards their house. Siya will be peeping and seeing if there is someone, she could not see anyone and then the white cat comes and pulls Siya's trouser meaning to step back. Then Siya steps back and takes the cat into her hands. Siya to cat: Aww, your so cute. Whose pet, are you? Will come home with me? And takes the cat inside the house everyone will love it except Smrithi and everyone will be playing with that cat and after some time they will have dinner and will leave to their rooms Siya goes to Smrithi's room and she will ask Smrithi to come and sleep with her in room. Then Smrithi will think for a while and she will tell okay to be with her in the room. Smrithi will be speaking on the phone and Siya will tell she will be walking for sometime in the balcony.

While Siya will be walking in the balcony she will here a knock on the gate and opens the gate and see there will be no one when she turns and see the whole road, she will see a boy standing under the street light.

She will think to go see him but the cat stops her so she ignores and starts listening to music and continue walking after sometime she will go back to her room to sleep by the time she goes Smrithi will be asleep. Siya will go and sleep next to her.

Siya also falls asleep thinking about the boy under the light. Around morning 4:00 am Smrithi will ask Siya to turn off the air conditioner then Siya will get up and turn off then starts walking towards the main gate Kyra will be watching Siya and runs towards her to stop her. Siya goes and opens the main gate and peeps out closes the gate and walk back towards her room by the time Kyra comes down. Kyra will search for Siya and she will not find her she will open the gate and see she will see the cat and "smiles and feels relief". She will be going back inside but she wanted to check if everything is fine so she will go near Siya's room she will see that black jacket boy and faint and fall there. After sometime Siya and Smrithi will wake up and when they come out off the room, they will see Kyra lying on the ground and run towards her to see if she is fine.

Siya: Hello, Kyra can you hear me? Kyra...

Kyra wakes up, Siya and Smrithi will start asking why she is here.

Siya: are you okay? Can you explain what happen to you?

Smrithi: Is your health fine?

Kyra (in stammering voice): I'm fine I wanted to speak to you girls so was coming to meet you but I slipped and feel down and was unconscious. That's all.

Smrithi: oh okay, here drink some water.

Kyra: yeah, thank you. I'll come and meet you later.

All the girls will be getting ready to visit their college and they will go visit and speak to their faculty and come back to home. Siya will tell Smrithi that she will go meet Kyra to check on her. Smrithi tells okay and goes to her room. Siya walks towards Kyra's home and see Kyra praying.

Kyra: Oh, God please help those girls and keep them safe they are innocent, please help them, don't give them any trouble.

Siya: what trouble?

Kyra: Hi dear, your back. How was the day in your new college?

Siya (strong suspicious tone): you were praying something for us what is it? What happen today morning?

Kyra (stammering voice): I told you right I slipped and fell unconscious.

Siya: You are hiding something, what's wrong what happen today.

Kyra: okay I'll tell you. And starts telling everything whatever happen in the morning.

Siya: why all these things are happening to us you know something about this but you are hiding.

Kyra (stammering voice): no that's it I don't know anything else

Siya: please tell me whatever you know. I'll try to solve it.

Kyra: Okay but...

| CAGED |

My inner child, trapped in my chest.
So much hurt, such little time to rest.
She cries and cries, spending the rest of her days away from all the lies.
She's tired of drowning in the sea of hate
Her little shoulders bear too much weight.

I reach out to her, but she makes me wait.
Looking at me with her beautiful brown eyes, They used to sparkle, once upon a time.
Staring at me, I could see, The rage and sadness Growing inside of her as she tells me her story. She doesn't use her voice, nor move her lips,
Not even a whisper to give me hints.
Just her eyes, they hold the emotions,
And that's enough to get me in motion.
So I sit by her, hoping my presence isn't a bother. Because no matter how much I reassure her,

-This pain, it's never truly over.

- Mahnoor

35

COLOURFUL MASHUP

Aastha Sharma

PERSEVERANCE

Inspired by a vision a soul sees every morning when it wakes up to see another day , in the time and dimension of this galaxy, it wonders if it would be able to make it to the old days, because it heard it's grandparents talk that" No wonder life is hard and with misery , every person should find small snippets because in those wrinkly skin and grey hair, there would be experiences worth seeing and living.

Parul Mangal

COLOR BURST

This beautiful painting has been entirely dot painted with acrylic paints requiring many hours of mindful focus, patience and devotion. Dot painting is a meditative process which reduces stress and calms the mind.

INTERVIEW

JOHN TRAPHAGAN

I'm an author and professor in the Department of Religious Studies and the Program in Human Dimensions of Organizations at the University of Texas at Austin. On this site, you will find links to my research related to Japan and to the ethics and culture of space exploration. You also will find information about my work as a jazz drummer and my role as host of the Science, Technology, and Society podcast channel on the New Books Network.

He indulged in a text interview with The Auctores.

- _How did you gravitate towards the field of writing? You're a teacher and researcher, is writing a repercussion of your profession ?_

●> _I've enjoyed writing since I was in middle school and perhaps because teachers often seemed to like my writing, the desire to write was reinforced. In college, I thought seriously about focusing on being a writer and I spent several years in the computer industry as a technical writer and editor, while also writing for newspapers and magazines as a freelancer. I did not find the technical writing and editing interesting and decided to return to graduate school at the University of Pittsburgh, where I received a PhD in anthropology. Writing is part of being a scholar. We do research and to disseminate the results we write articles and books. Most academic writing, however, is of poor quality in terms of prose, even if it presents good research. Because I enjoy the craft of writing, I have tried to bring a writer's approach and mind to my academic publications._

- _Could you tell our readership what values you try to inculcate in your writings? Introduce them to your newest publication. what do you often find yourself writing about ?_

●> I've written about many things over the course of my career, but the thread that brings these things together is that there is a focus on how humans bring a diverse set of values and ideas to their world and that there is no single way of seeing the world that is true. My latest book, Embracing Uncertainty: Future Jazz, That 13th Century Buddhist Monk, and the Invention of Cultures, is something of an anthropological memoir that goes into detail about how living in and deeply learning about other cultures generates a basic uncertainty which is, I think, something we need to embrace rather than something to be pushed away. I weave together ideas from philosophers such as Richard Rorty, the Zen monk Dōgen, and my own experience as an anthropologist to explore the contingent nature of our experience. A key idea of the book is that clinging to the desire for certainty actually causes many of our problems and also is a significant source of suffering. This is probably the most basic value I hold as a person and shapes the way I see and experience the world.

- You have been to many places around the world. Which place did you like the most and which had the most influence on your life ?

●> I've been fortunate to travel all over the world, but I don't think I can really describe one place as that which I like the most. I really don't think of the world that way. Instead, I think most places have interesting things to offer and there is great value in trying to understand life from the perspectives of the people who live in those places. The place that has most influenced me, outside of the US, is Japan. I've spent a total of about five years in Japan and I find the approach to life there appealing, particularly in the more rural areas. There is a much stronger sense of personal responsibility as well as concern for the well-being of others than I find in the US. Where I see the US as an exceedingly self-oriented society in which many people feel a strong sense of entitlement, I see Japan as a much more other-oriented society in which people care about the needs of those they encounter on a daily basis and often put those needs ahead of their own desires. Like any place, there are many different types of people in Japan, including very selfish people, but the culture as a whole puts an emphasis on being less focused on "me" than I see in American culture.

- You're a vividly skilled person and have worked on several gigs which assume different roles, which of these roles do you happen to like the most ?

●> This a nice comment. Thank you. I'm not sure I can really answer this question. I do not think about things I like in this sort of comparative way. I tend to live as much as possible in the present and avoid comparison of what I'm doing now with what I might have been doing in the past. Nor do I think much about the future. I've never been one for setting goals in life. I think the quality of experience in an action or role is something you bring to that role. The more you are able to stay focused on what you are doing in the moment, the more it will be "enjoyable." But, again, I don't spend a lot of time thinking about what is enjoyable.

- Can you please share with us your best childhood memory ? And how was it spending your childhood in Massachusetts, how did it shape you ?

●> This is a similar problem to the previous question. I very rarely look backward in life. My past is past. It's gone. Nothing about it can be changed, so I see little point in dwelling on the past or even thinking about it much. I also have a rather poor memory for past things—I often have no idea what I did five days ago, let alone five years ago. What I can say is that when I was in high school, I belonged to a nationally ranked drum and bugle corps called the 27th Lancers. I was fortunate to tour across the US performing in front of many people. The corps taught me discipline and focus. It taught me to work hard and to get things done without complaining. We had a corps motto that was "do it, do it now." I live by that motto to this day.

• Now, maybe the most important question of our interview session. How do you write a book ? Our readership comprises of some amazing writers and artists, I'm certain many of them aspire to become successful writers, so what tip or advice would you like to share with them ?

●> My approach to writing is weird. Most of what you are told to do by people who teach writing are things I don't do. For example, I never write an outline. I find that if I write an outline, it tends to restrict my thinking—I use writing as a means to think, so I want to have flexibility in my thought patterns. Outlines get in the way of that for me. So I just start writing and see where the ideas go. I let the story or argument take me where it needs to go as I am writing. I also write in very short bursts of extremely intense activity. I wrote my last book in about three weeks. The book I have coming out in September took a little longer than that, but I wrote 20,000 words in one weekend. This sort of intensity allows me to become completely absorbed in the writing. I basically live in the world—whether fiction or non-fiction—that I am writing. I wake up at 3am with ideas running through my head and write them immediately. I'm not very communicative when this is happening, which is a bit of a pain for my family, but they seem to tolerate it.

As for advice, I think there are a few things that are important. First, the best way to improve at writing is to read—and read a lot. The more you read, the more you come to understand how other authors approach their craft and that influences what you do in your own writing. Second, write. Just write a lot and your writing will develop. However, it won't do so in a vacuum, which brings me to the third and most important point. You must be open to constructive criticism. Do not be afraid of negative comments on your work and do not dismiss those who dislike something you have written. Learn from their comments and try to develop your craft using what you learn. This does not, however, mean that you have to agree with every critique you read or hear. I'll give you an example. Sometimes I will get a comment that a sentence or paragraph is difficult to follow. I read it, and I don't agree; it seems entirely clear to me. I could ignore that comment, but instead I ask, "okay, if this person couldn't make sense out of my writing, there is probably a way I can improve this passage to ensure it is more easily understood." I may think the passage is clear, but someone didn't get it, so there must be a better way to write it. Constructive criticism makes your writing improve. Sometimes even not particularly constructive criticism can be useful. The worst thing for me is to be told, "wow, that is just amazing! I love it! You are such a great writer!" It feels nice to hear that sort of thing, but it doesn't actually help me improve my craft.

- *I would like to know how you came to be a professor in the Department of Religious studies. And how is your experience as a professor ?*

●> *I am trained as a cultural anthropologist and I have done quite a bit of research on religion in Japan. I was located in Asian Studies at my university when the Department of Religious Studies was created. Because my research had strong connections with Japanese religion, I decided to move to the new department. I enjoy teaching and research. Teaching is tremendously rewarding. I think I generally learn a lot more from my students than they learn from me, and I truly enjoy a good classroom in which people are developing and debating their ideas. The one part of my job as a professor I dislike is administrative work. I tend to enjoy things that involved creativity and I find no creativity in administrative work. Perhaps it's there, but I don't' see it. I find it tedious and boring and administrators often seem to be just making busy work so that they can appear useful. I'm also very much an introvert and a loner, so I do not particularly enjoy working closely with others unless they are individuals with whom I can find a strong connection.*

- *You've spent your time researching about Tohoku, Japan. How did the idea come through and was it always a plan ? Tell us a few things about Tohoku and what you liked most about it.*

●> *My reason for doing research in that area is probably not what one would expect. My wife is from that region of Japan and when I decided to go back to graduate school and study Japan it seemed to make sense to study the area where she grew up. My early research was on aging and dementia in Japan and that region has a large population of older people. Also, but a very strange coincidence, my dissertation advisor, L. K. Brown, had been doing research in the town where my wife went to high school for many years. She had never run across him, but the connection seemed oddly opportune. So, no, it wasn't part of a plan; it just sort of happened by accident. But I would describe most of my life that way. I've never planned much of anything—most of my life has just been one interesting accident after another. I go with the flow and enjoy finding out, and writing about, the interesting things I discover along the way.*

Visit **www.sites.utexas.edu/john-traphagan**
to know more about John and his works.

COLOUR PUNCH

Kay.

Surekha Biswas

THEN I THOUGHT,

WHY NOT LIVE A LITTLE?

| BROKEN |

Continued after chapter 4

CHAPTER 5

I went home and as early as possible I hid my scars. It wasn't that I didn't want to tell Appa. It's just that I was scared. I was scared for what was about to come. I knew very well from where they all belonged too, their rich parents and all of those kids a couple of spoiled brats...

If I got parents involved it is going to be big. I'll just try to ignore them and see what could they really do. Not that I couldn't fight back but it's going to enrage them more. They're going to enjoy hurting me. I won't tell Appa, Giving it a last and final thought I did my homework and went to bed early that day.

NEXT DAY:

I woke up before Appa and after having some breakfast and getting ready, I went out early leaving a note on the fridge. I went to the park, wrote on my journal, and was off to school when Ava found me. She grabbed my wrist suddenly and I gasped.

"Huh! Oh my god, is this bruise because of me? Oh lord! I'm so sorry! So-"She started mumbling and stuttering, A habit of hers. "Hey..hey!It's not because of you. I just fell yesterday on my back to home, nothing much."

After taking a look at my bruise she let go of my hand and continued her walk towards school mumbling an "if you say so"...

Throughout classes, Elena kept on glaring at me...

And I was just hiding my face trying not to be caught by her.It was about recess time when I was about to get up someone left a note on my table stating

"Come on the rooftop. If you don't, you know the consequences...I have your video and ps...come alone ;)"

I knew it was Elena and her friends. And I had no choice.

"You guys go ahead, I'll be back." Both of them nodded and I took my footsteps towards the rooftop mentally preparing myself for what was about to come.

Opening a door I was greeted by a bucket of water mixed with black paint falling on me ...

"Oh wow!!! You actually came. I thought We had to send someone to drag you up here. Come here! sit by us." Austin spoke up. I followed what he said.

Everyone, there was smirking, most probably laughing at my miserable state meanwhile I was like a deer caught in headlights...

- Urvah

"Eat all of this," He said handing me a box full of pastries. I simply shook my head."
HUH? You cannot say no to your friends, right? Here, be a good girl and eat it" he
said bringing a pastry to my mouth. I didn't open my mouth and he forcefully shoved all
of the pastry at once...

There was red chili in that pastry and everyone started laughing about completing their
mission. I have a spice allergy. Elena knows it very clearly. If I take spice more than
my toleration I get sick and most often faint...Tears were streaming down my face and
I was asking for water but no one, no one was there...

"Here, have some more!"Elena now shoved one in my face.

And I cried harder. I tried a million times to stop her. Those lackeys of her took my
hands."WATER!"I screamed

"Oh she needs water, give her some "

Austin took a water bottle and threw it on my face. "Here, drink as much as you
want.."They all laughed.

The whole day I sat on the rooftop, not attending any of the class, and was crying
continuously. The school ended. Ava and Tina were calling and texting me continuously
asking me where I was.I told them I was okay and to go home.

Going down and getting my bag on the way I ended one more awful day of school.
Telling myself that everything's okay and I'll be alright, I went back home.

Appa called asking me If I was okay and that he had a feeling as if someone close to
me was sad. He said that his soul's so anxious.

I wanted to tell him that it is because of me and I wanted to cry so bad. I wanted to
hug him tight but I couldn't. I want to scream all of my worries into the phone but I
couldn't. It was as if the world around me was crying but only I could listen to it. My
ears and eyes were tired from it and I wanted to end it. But I couldn't.

| WHAT YOU SEEK IS SEEKING YOU |

You're searching for home desparately racing against yourself,
racing against time as if not claimed today, you'll lose it all.
But the truth is,
in a quiet corner somewhere beyond all of this hustle,
race and competition, your home is waiting for you too.

- Ayushi Parulekar

43

| PHONY RIVER |

I wanted to dive in the ocean that people hide beside their running river, just like i hide mine behind a phoney river,

There were the days when i waited to noticed, desperatly wanted someone to dive in my ocean to understand the depths, the struggle, the suffering of my ocean but as the days passed i realized that people only like to damp their toes in the rivers. They only like to sit on the shore not dare to dive and feel the depths or endure the others ocean not because they're ignorant or don't care but because they're too gasping and trying to save theirselves from their own ocean of labyrinth, they are too trying to be alive from their own drowning ocean, but sometimes they swim so far in their ocean that they reach someone else and then they realized they're not alone who's struggling, they aren't the one who have drowning ocean beside the river that they only let people to see. And now i realized there are thousands of oceans that people hide inside.

- Atika ilyas

| PHANTOM |

This world, it's a mirage, the people, are merely masked mannequins, and the reality is overwhelming. The friend is a foe, the devils are in the disguise of angels. The whole world is a mystery. Nobody is trustable, none of us. There are double-sided people, one day rude, another day sweet, but no one knows what's going on in their head. Then some people pretend to be friends, just for the sake of friendship. Some people ditch friendship at the last moment and leave you alone when you need them the most. Life is quite unpredictable. How abruptly it takes turns. How one day you are the happiest person on the whole planet, and the next day, the most gloomy one. How humanity seems to be a curse when one takes advantage of your kindness. How people take no time to break to your heart and make it bleed for years.How one wrong decision ruins your whole life. And the sand of your life keeps slipping away from your hands. The clock seems to tick more quickly than ever. The seasons seem to change in no time, and you still wait eagerly for the moment, which had already gone. It's all quite intriguing and seems delusional, but it's the reality. You still stand, from where you started, but this time with a smile, after catching a glimpse of the vicious yet real world.

- Diya Jain

INTERVIEW

I'm a twenty-something poet from the UK and the author of three books. I have a degree in English Language & Linguistics and I began writing poetry in September 2018. I published my debut book, Moonflower, in February 2020. Divided into three chapters (Wilt, Grow, and Bloom), it is an illustrated poetry collection about learning to grow even through darkness. I then worked with Quarto Publishing to create a guided poetry journal designed to encourage and inspire others to have a go at writing poetry.

She indulged in a text interview with The Auctores.

- Tell us something about your newest publication ?

●> My latest book is called All This Wild Hope. It's a poetry collection divided into three chapters: longing, learning, and healing, which explore the different kinds of hope - the hope we long for, the hope we learn to find, and the hope that heals us. This book covers topics such as mental health, self-love, healing, love, forgiveness, courage, and recovery.

- How did you come up with your debut book? Was it always a plan or something that happened along the way?

●> I knew early on that I wanted to put together a poetry collection, but I was unsure about the theme and title for a while. Instead of dwelling on it too much, I just kept writing poetry and realised after a while that many of them fit into a theme of light and dark, and growing through both of them. I knew then that I wanted the book to follow a black and white interior theme, and after working as a freelance illustrator and tattoo designer for a few years, I was keen to add illustrations. One day, I read something about moonflowers and how they bloom at night, and I realised it fit perfectly with the theme of the poems I was writing. Everything then fell into place.

- As a linguistic student what advice do you have to offer to the newcomers in the writing industry and how should they be prepared?

●> Don't be afraid of rejection, don't be afraid to share your words, and don't worry about the number of followers you have on social media.

- In your opinion how does contemporary writings differ from the classic ones? Isn't today's contemporary going to become tomorrow's classic ?

●> Modern poetry uses a lot less poetic and linguistic techniques compared to classic poetry. Modern poetry is more straightforward, whereas with classic poetry you often have to search a lot deeper to find hidden meanings. This can be a good thing, however, because it makes it more accessible. They are both beautiful in their own way!

- How much your career today is influenced from your childhood upbringing and the place you spent your days as a kid ?

●> My parents greatly influenced my love of books - when I was a young child my mother would read me a bedtime story every night. Then, once I was a little older, we would go to our local library every weekend to get a book. I also loved writing as a child and would fill countless notepads with stories. I think moving to the countryside at 11 years old also ignited a love of nature which has inspired many of my poems.

- You published your debut book recently, how much of a task it was getting yourself published ? How hard it was on a scale of 1 to 10.

●> It can vary - I would say All This Wild Hope was 3 out of 10, and Moonflower was 6. But that's only because I had some problems with the illustrations in Moonflower which made it a slightly tricker process. Overall, it's pretty easy to self publish a book. I used Amazon's KDP publishing service for both my poetry collections. Once you have everything sorted, it only takes 5 minutes to actually publish your book. They have lots of helpful information and they guide you through the process step by step. It's also completely free to publish, but they do take a 40% royalty as well as printing costs. I would also highly recommend paying for an editor/proofreader, and a cover design, as these things will make your book seem much more professional.

- Point out something that you didn't like about the creative industry. Provided the chance how would you like to change this thing?

●> There isn't much I would change, actually! It's a very supportive and talented community.

- Now, maybe the most important question of our interview session.How do you write a book ? Our readership comprises of some amazing writers and artists, I'm certain many of them aspire to become successful writers, so what tip or advice would you like to share with them ?

●> Read a lot in the genre you want to write in. Write as often as you can. Stop comparing yourself to others. Write for yourself and not what you think others want to hear. Just go for it!

My second poetry collection was released this June and is entitled *All This Wild Hope*. This collection exlores the different kinds of hope - the hope we long for, the hope we learn to find, and the hope that heals us. It is a reminder to find hope in the smallest places and hold it close.

| COFFEE AND RAIN |

Oh! it was cruel summer
with hot springs
and boring violins.
After five days with empty sky,
There is clouds in the sky,
In the month of july.
Thunder in our hearts,
Cheerfulness in the parks.
Oh, see it started to rain.
Puddles on the road,
Make your vehicles slowed.
Don't get explode,
in the excitement.
Come dance with me ,
under the rainbow.
Don't say no.
How dazzling is the rain,
Oh! don't worry, it will come again.
After the dust and heat,
The raindrops will meet our feet.
And that will be sweet.
What's better than Coffee and rain.
Oh! don't worry, it will come again.

– Khushi Bhola

48

| THIS I FEAR |

How easy it is to walk those halls of blue and grey
but how difficult it be to see them
As they shimmer their silver // serenely
enchanted spires to rise
arisen above celestial sea //
Her expanses of murky mist,
whose far-reaches have seen
history woven in history
Century upon century

A hinterland unfolded;
and the grey of body grey of mist
in unity; I do not fear it in myself,
I do not fear its lot
I have touched it before,
though only its shallow spaces //
I fear it in others and what be left behind —
A duller blue, a hungrier blue
// the disunited husk of the blue,
which washes upon our earthly shores
To wash away and leave but remnants,
trinkets and tales
come once and gone

this I fear.

– Alicia Buckeridge

49

WHAT IS MINDFULNESS ?

DANA ABOU ZEKI

Nowadays, due to the fast paced and information overload environment we live in, most of us operate under what we call the "autopilot mode". It is a state in which we have a vague awareness of what is happening in the present moment, we are hardly aware of what is occurring around us (sounds, sights, smells, etc.) and what is occurring within us (physical, mental and emotional sensations). We do things without much thought, we behave in a mechanical way and we do so without awareness! This is what we call the "autopilot mode" and "Mindfulness" is the exact opposite of that!

Mindfulness is our ability to maintain moment by moment awareness of what is happening around us, and what is happening within us (our body sensations, feelings and thoughts)! It is simply being fully present in the current moment which allows us to have control over our emotions and in essence is the core of Emotional Intelligence.

It helps us to pause, reflect then decide how to act, cultivating an awareness of changes in our emotional and physical sensations!

Jon Kabat-Zinn, the founder of Mindfulness Based Stress Reduction (MBSR), defines mindfulness as "paying attention in a particular way; on purpose, in the present moment, and non-judgmentally.", so mindfulness is a decision that one takes! To decide to pay attention in a particular way, to observe what is happening around us and within us without judgement requires practice and commitment. It is a journey and the more we practice mindfulness and make it part of our daily lives, the more we become the non-judgmental observers of our patterns of thinking and emotions and as a result we become clearer on what action needs to be taken or not!

Mindfulness helps us cultivate a state of awareness, in which we are fully present in the

moment and we learn to leave behind our tendency to judge a situation, circumstance, decision or person (which usually causes issues and conflicts). So, mindfulness gives us the freedom to respond rather than react, gives us the tools we need to step out of autopilot mode and think things through before we say or do something that we might regret!

There are many benefits of mindfulness, below are some of the scientifically tested ones:

Ø   Increase in productivity and creativity

Ø   Better sleep

Ø   Increase in the level of focus

Ø   Decrease in stress

Ø   Decrease in anxiety

Ø   May help treat depression

Ø   Improves cognition

Ø   Improves attention

Ø   Help the brain reduce distractions

So where is mindfulness today ?

Mindfulness programs were first developed in the 1970s. A Mindfulness based stress reduction program was developed at the University of Massachusetts Medical Center in the 1970s by Professor Jon Kabat-Zinn, MBSR uses a combination of mindfulness meditation, body awareness, yoga and exploration of patterns of behavior, thinking, feeling and action. And after that many other programs were developed such as MBCT (Mindfulness Based Cognitive therapy) which is a more focused therapy and is an approach to psychotherapy that uses CBT with mindfulness meditative practices. (developed to treat severe cases of depression and anxiety). Today mindfulness programs have gone beyond clinical work and therapy sessions, mindfulness programs are being applied in schools and at work. The UK, has now included mindfulness as part of their school curriculum and many companies such as Google, Linked-in to name a few are investing heavily in mindfulness programs.

Dana is a certified mindfulness coach and meditation and yoga teacher with an open heart to spread wellness, happiness, and health by teaching mindfulness and meditation techniques that will help others manage and decrease their stress levels to allow them to have a more balanced life. Dana believes that stress is the main cause of illness, hoping to raise awareness on the importance of investing in wellness for a healthier and happier life!

Mindfulness is a way of living, a choice, a decision one takes towards his wellbeing, it allows us to feel and value what is important in life and provides us with the tools we need to live a happy and less stressed life!

How mindful are you?

Visit www.mindfulvedana.com to know more about Dana and Mindfullness.

| GRAIL |

The symbology of the simple hits me
There's not much to look around here
The quiet life sometimes chokes the soul
me and you
That you run away between my fingers and you knock me down in fear
There is no voluptuousness in what I tell you
Or even some
However
The charm is rare and
so full of affection
Exile among the puddles of infinite love
Calculate that you who have never seen him
Dust between gaps that reach you in depth
If I go, I exercise in thinking
That this way of loving is vile
I'm no longer a goddess in execution
rhetorical perfita in reason
Oh God, see me as mortal
why when dying
I be the tear that will give life to the end of your days

~ Neide Laura Lopes

52

| IN MY MIRROR |

I've been looking for her,
expecting to see her at the corner
of a random street,
yet she's way too discreet.

People told me that she's rare to find,
but I hope I would be fine
if I kept on searching,
if I kept on moving and exploring

either through mini adventures,
by learning a new culture,
I even travelled far away,
hoping that one day

I'd be able to find her,
that she'd stand in the crowd,
yet she's nowhere to be found,
I've been searching for a few years.

I even thought I'd meet her if I exercised,
if I lost weight, if I looked slimmer,
but 3 years later I have realised
that confidence only exists in my mirror.

– Shiva

PROMPT BATTLE

FREEDOM

Freedom for me is travelling at night
Without any fear
Not sending location while sitting in a taxi
Not being sandwiched between elders and
generation z
My identity My legacy not just a
daughter, wife , mom!
This freedom I aspire for !

- Rekha

The day of freedom.
The day of triumph.
The day to cheer.
For our country so special and dear.
Cherish the day with enthusiasm.
Freedom is the greatest gift to mankind.
Freedom costs blood.
The birds flying in the sky,
are cherishing peace and love.
Our country sacrificed many warriors.
Independence is their blessings for us.
As we all Indians
We are a Nation.
We don't have any religion.
We speak the language of love.
We stand with kindness and blood.
By giving a tribute to the motherland, all we can do
is live with peace and tranquility.

- Khushi

PROMPT BATTLE

RIGHT

Right and Wrong they say are the two faces of coin
For you if its heads, with tail I'll join...
If I see from thy eyes
You see from mine
I sense the love dies
When right and wrong is in our minds

-Inked Photography

I drew a line today, a fracture in space. The reason, a simple request. To stop being repository for other's needs and feelings. I will struggle to understand. Those who treats their every thought as sanctified. To never check for connection. Never check for positive engagement. Never check into the soul to the person to who they are speaking. We are all singular entities who want to feel loved. So more tempestuously then intended. I pushed back directly. It was empty in acceptance. I hate what the ladt of my energy tends to do.

- Genevieve Ray

|| श्री भगवद गीता ||

अध्याय 1 श्लोक 12-14

तस्य सञ्जनयन्हर्षं कुरुवृद्धः पितामहः ।

सिंहनादं विनद्योच्चैः शंख दध्मो प्रतापवान् ।।1.12।।

ततः शंखाश्च भेर्यश्च पणवानकगोमुखाः ।

सहसैवाभ्यहन्यन्त स शब्दस्तुमुलोऽभवत् ।।1.13।।

ततः श्वेतैर्हयैर्युक्ते महति स्यन्दने स्थितौ ।

माधवः पाण्डवश्चैव दिव्यौ शंखौ प्रदध्मतुः ।।1.14।।

कौरवों में वृद्ध बड़े प्रतापी पितामह भीष्म ने उस दुर्योधन के हृदय में हर्ष उत्पन्न करते हुए उच्च स्वर से सिंह की दहाड़ के समान गरजकर शंख बजाया. इसके पश्चात शंख और नगाड़े तथा ढोल, मृदंग और नरसिंघे आदि बाजे एक साथ ही बज उठे। उनका वह शब्द बड़ा भयंकर हुआ. इसके अनन्तर सफेद घोड़ों से युक्त उत्तम रथ में बैठे हुए श्रीकृष्ण महाराज और अर्जुन ने भी अलौकिक शंख बजाए ।

|| श्री भगवद गीता ||

इस अध्याय के आरंभ में धृतराष्ट्र ने संजय से पूछा था की युद्ध क्षेत्र में मेरे और पांडु के पुत्रों ने क्या किया? अतः संजय ने दूसरे श्लोक से थरेहवी श्लोक तक धृतराष्ट्र के पुत्रों ने क्या किया इसका उत्तर दिया आगे के श्लोकों से संजय पांडु के पुत्रों ने क्या किया उसका उत्तर देते हैं।

तो 12 वे श्लोक में ये बताया है कि भीष्म जी ने शंखनाद किया कुरु वंश के वृद्ध पितामह अपने पौत्र दुर्योधन का मनोभाव जान गए और उसके प्रति अपनी स्वाभाविक दया दिखाते हुए उन्होंने उसे प्रसन्न करने के लिए अत्यंत उच्च स्वर में अपना शंख बजाया जो उनकी सिंह के समान स्थिति के अनुरूप था । इसका एक मतलब यह भी निकलता है कि दुर्योधन द्वारा चालाकी से कही गई बातों का द्रोणाचार्य ने कोई उत्तर नहीं दिया। उन्होंने यही समझा कि दुर्योधन चालाकी से उनको ठगना चाहता है । इसलिए वह भी चुप ही रहे परंतु पितामह (दादा) होने के नाते भीष्म जी ने दुर्योधन की चलाकि मैं उनका बचपना देखते है अतः पितामह भीष्म द्रोणाचार्य के समान चुप न रह कर वात्सल्य (प्रेम) भाव के कारण दुर्योधन को हर्षित करते हुए शंख बजाते हैं जैसे सिंह के गर्जना करने पर हाथी आदि बड़े-बड़े पशु भी भयभीत हो जाते हैं ऐसी ही गर्जना करने मात्र से सभी भयभीत हो जाए और दुर्योधन प्रसन्न हो जाए इसी भाव से भीष्म सिंह के समान गरज कर जोर से शंख बजाया। इसके बाद नगाड़े, बिगुल, तुरई तथा सिंग सब एक साथ बज उठे है वह समस्त स्वर अत्यंत कोलाहल पूर्ण था ।

इसके बाद दूसरे छोर से अर्जुन और कृष्ण भी अपनी अपने दिव्य शंख बजाते हैं भीष्म देव द्वारा बजाए गए शंख की तुलना में कृष्ण तथा अर्जुन के शंखो को दिव्य कहा गया है दिव्य शंखों के नाद से यह सूचित हो रहा था कि दूसरे पक्ष की विजय की कोई आशा नहीं थी जो कि कृष्ण पांडवों के पक्ष में थे और जहां जहां भगवान विद्यमान हैं वहीं वहीं लक्ष्मी जी भी रहती हैं क्योंकि वह अपने पति के बिना नहीं रह सकती अतः जैसा कि विष्णु अथवा भगवान कृष्ण के शंख द्वारा उत्पन्न दिव्य धनी से सूचित हो रहा था विजय तथा श्री दोनों ही अर्जुन की प्रतीक्षा कर रही थी।

|| श्री भगवद गीता ||

At the beginning of this chapter, Dhritarashtra asked Sanjaya what did my sons and Pandu's sons do in the battle field? So Sanjaya answered what Dhritarashtra's sons did from the second verse to the thirehavi verse. From the next verses, Sanjaya answers what Pandu's sons did.

So in the 12th verse it is told that Bhishma ji made a conch was in a similar situation. This also means that Dronacharya did not give any answer to the cleverly said things by Duryodhana. They understood that Duryodhana was cleverly trying to cheat them. That's why he also remained silent, but being the grandfather (grandfather) Bhishma told Duryodhana that I see his childhood, so grandfather Bhishma does not remain silent like Dronacharya and blows conch shell to please Duryodhana due to the feeling of Vatsalya (love). Just as big animals like elephants get frightened when a lion roars, in the same way, everyone should be frightened by the mere roar and Duryodhana should be pleased, with the same feeling, Bhishma roared like a lion and blew conch shell loudly. After this the drums, bugle, trumpet and sing all rang together, that whole voice was very noisy.

After this, Arjun and Krishna also blow their own divine conch from the other end. There was no hope that Krishna was on the side of the Pandavas and where the Lord is present, Lakshmi ji also lives there because she cannot live without her husband so as indicated by the divine riches produced by the conch shell of Vishnu or Lord Krishna. Both Vijay and Sri were waiting for Arjuna.

- Compiled by Shubh Kaushik

CREDITS

Designs by @gargkuku

Cover by @aaronwilcoxgalleries

@ccwritess
@sageofdawn
@candour_at_core
@nisha.mnisha
@theinkthought_
@kiki_poetry
@heymonthninja
@traceydoesrhymetime
@_.sudikshaartfeeds._
@anastasiasmithart
@enigma_sq
@wanna_bee_poet
@bg_babsauthor
@snehakannusamy
@makinde_kehinde_margret
@jellybeantoespoetry
@booksandsejuti
@shwetamahani
@hayatt.askim
@_a.dzzzz_
@_aesthetic.secrets_
@_unique_infusion
@s.l.b.rambling
@gothrulz
@swati_mishra_0
@uncoverthisworld
@shuchibatra.poetry
@untethered_wings
@yachnaa_10

@the_sophisticatedteen
@renaria.b.poetry
@of_brushesandbruises
@christian_ward_writes
@sd.hades
@kayderaart
@greetjesiekmans
@mystical._.hazel
@nikhita.k15
@bxbumblebee
@creationsbyparul
@john_traphagan
@_aesthetic.secrets_
@excerpts_from_my_existence
@happywords__
@aatikas_pov
@poeticreign_
@sabinalaurapoetry
@dawn.to_dusk
@faerie_aliciabeatrice
@mindfulvedana
@nllwriter
@shiva.poems
@dilserekha
@inked.photograph
@genevievefirepoet
@shubh_chetna

Thanks for recognising the effort put into this journal.

YOU CAN SEND YOUR WORKS FOR OUR UPCOMING EDITIONS BY SCANNING THE QR BELOW

THE AUCTORES MONTHLY SUBMISSION FORM

Scan this QR code to access our submission form.

DONATE TO US

We accept and require generous donations from capable philanthropists, artists and authors to continuously submit to the growth of contemporary Creatives around the globe through diversified means in ARTS and LITERATURE.
We support budding creatives (artists, authors and photo artists) by sharing their work through our various platforms like social media and monthly editorials.
We're a non profit entity dedicated to help authors and artists of today and therefore anyone who is looking for our support or looking to get their work published in one of our editorials isn't charged any fee. What matters for us is only the quality of content you share using our platforms.

 Scan this QR code to make a donation to us.

Printed in Great Britain
by Amazon